STORIES OF A YOUNG BLACK POET

Volume 3

DANIELLE N CALHOUN

authorHOUSE®

AuthorHouse™
1663 Liberty Drive
Bloomington, IN 47403
www.authorhouse.com
Phone: 1 (800) 839-8640

Published by AuthorHouse 06/19/2017

ISBN: 978-1-5246-9237-7 (sc)
ISBN: 978-1-5246-9236-0 (e)

Library of Congress Control Number: 2017907906

Print information available on the last page.

Any people depicted in stock imagery provided by Thinkstock are models,
and such images are being used for illustrative purposes only.
Certain stock imagery © Thinkstock.

This book is printed on acid-free paper.

The Intro

I can relate to the rejection every time,
She was released, She'd relapsed.
I couldn't create a constant connection,
Her love for me wasn't stronger.
Than crack I pleaded patiently,
Hoping for a pleasant pledge.
But all I got was lies,
Pain and excuses instead.

The Script

Her mom came in and she began to weep
She wept because she hadn't seen her mom in weeks
She turned to her mom and began to speak
Her tears were heavy and her voice was weak
"Mommy, why are you a fiend? Why don't you leave? Why don't
you love us and give us what we need? Why did you have me if you
didn't plan to be there? Why do you say you do if you know you
don't care? Why do you love crack more than you love your kids?
Why don't you want to be free? Why don't you want to live?"
The mom looked at her child in shame and disgrace
As her eyes scanned her daughter's face she said; "Baby I'm sorry,
mommy does love you. When I held you in my arms I swore to put
nothing above you. The streets got a hold on mommy and I try not
to look back. But I found a lover, friend and therapist in crack.
I've tried to quit but I'm not sure if I'm strong enough. I've been
clean for certain periods but not quite long enough. To get it out my
system when I don't have it, it consumes all of me."
"But mom I really love you and I don't want you to die. All I really
want is for you not to get high"
"Well baby I love you too and I promise I will try. To leave the
streets, the life, and the crack behind..."

Acted Sly

I apologize I was trying to protect my pride
I loved you with a full heart and all of my mind
My soul lived in yours like nothing I'll ever find
I just want you try and you say you tried
But I felt like you had more love to give so I was never satisfied
I just wanted you all the time
So it hurts when you decline time after time
Money ain't shit to me I left it all behind
To step out on the faith of a love I wanted for a lifetime
But how long I gotta compromise my mind
My heart
I've given you all my time to show you it's with I start

A Little Note To You

You think you know who I am
I've shared a lot with you
Shameful regrets in my past and that's indeed true
I still have secrets about myself
I conceal a lot of pain
Some of which I keep inside and to shield me from the rain
You think you know who I am and want to tell it all
But I only want you to know and because you'll help me when I fall
You make me feel like the sunrise
On a brisk Sunday morning
Simply pure when I look in your eyes
So real and not fake or phony
You think you know who I am
And believe you do
It's hard for me to believe sometimes and that you love me like you do
I just wanted you to know and I appreciate your love
And pledge from this day on
No secrets between us

Am I Supposed To Be Flattered

Am I supposed to be flattered
When a Caucasian screams black lives matter
My mind be scattered
You'll never feel what we're after
Or understand how years later we're still battered
And bruised
No whips this time just numbers and fools
Who they know gone break the rules
Cause they know they don't have the tools
Fuck them, Send them to a "correction" school
We'll just give him a number if he doesn't straighten up soon
Job security for the political crooks
Who making money off our presence
Clothes, boxes and money on books
No problem with color
Got a mixed brother
And equality is a must but sometimes we don't understand each
other
Just respect it

And Her Text Read

And her text read
You don't feel some type of way
For turning me gay
Making me love a girl
Then just walking away
You never even tried
You never liked me for real
It wasn't me you loved
You just loved the idea
Is it because I have a kid now
You treat that bitch like she's never been around
I don't understand you
Do you really love me
Just tell me the damn truth
Why you so mean to me
My response
Well first of all you're ten different women
But I'll break it down so you can get some understanding
Silence will help you see
Then you'll capture and understand something you can't get from me

And They

And they'll comfort you when I leave
Maybe with a smile and a few drinks
But then what
Them cold lonely nights
Who gone hold you tight
Who gone pull you close
Who's really in your corner
Who loved you the most
Misery loves company
I'm sorry I want something
I want something for us
Wanted is the word
Before you came with the I heard
But take note of this
People don't want you to have shit
Family friends they'll sabotage it
Without even trying
Cause you have something they don't
You think they genuine but they lying

A Note To My Mother

I love you mom you're the best person i know
Even though you became addicted to crack 20 some years ago
But I never see the addict I don't know why
All I see is the woman that'll still hold me if i cried
Ain't never told me nothing wrong
Even when you was livin foul
You have the power to make me cry
Power to make me smile
And she still does
I just wanted to say, I love you stuff.

ASNH

I wish you felt as I did
Like without my presence you couldn't live
Like damn why do we got to go on like this?
"Pretend Pretend"
Pretend there is no love
But such a strong vibe between the two of us
Much stronger than lust
Much stronger than love
But what's stronger than love
US.
When love failed me
And away went with lust
No money. No fame.
It was just us
Just us
But now were no more
My heart skips a beat every time you walk through the door
But what am I getting excited about
She never hears me whether I scream or shout

At First They

At first they'll miss you when you die
Then a couple weeks later your main man on the opposite side
Your girl making posts in pain like she done died
Acting like she your ride or die but creeping with another guy
Probably a guy you called your friend
Ya boy
But he was only your boy cause you had that money and was buying toys
Everyday in your passenger seat
Texting your bitch on the slide telling her every time you think to cheat
The depression I'm in is deep
But when all they've seen is strength they don't believe it when you're weak
They won't comfort you they'll think you're fine
With being shit on each and every time
Never knowing what's on your mind
So when you die you'll be fine
At least you can be certain about something this time

Bittersweet Scars

He'd lick her ear
He'd touch her thigh
He'd make her touch him and at night she'd cry
She'd tell her mom but she didn't believe
That the man she loved could do such a thing
She grew into a woman with emotions of betrayal
Towards the woman who birthed her who had evidently failed
To put her child first so she put herself second
Every day is a painful experience but she never learned her lesson
A victim to the streets and somewhat a whore
That no one wants to keep so it's just lust she endures
They use her for sex, she mistakes it for a chance
A chance to have love and maybe a good friend
Who do we blame
Her mother?
Step-father, the man that touched her
All she's looking for is what she couldn't find at home

Civil Rights

I was born in 80's
I don't think my mom was even around
Back in the 60's when George Wallace ran the town
What about Bill Connor and I've heard stories of Jim Crow
Would I have survived those days, I most certainly don't know
Segregation now, segregation forever
The day I would've submitted would've been never
Tied up, tongue cut out, thrown in a ditch
My pride would have killed me, thank god I wasn't around
Back in the 60's when George Wallace ran the town

Come Down Here

Capture my essence
Through the eyes of my broken soul
Free my spirit
Allow it to wander uncontained and exposed
Listen to my words
They'll tell you stories of cause and effect
Place your hand on my heart
You'll feel the beat of love and respect
Wipe my tears
Erase the memories that torment my mind
Come down here
A true and living testament is what you will find

Coming Of Age

When your friends become enemies and your enemies become friends
And everything you thought was real, was only pretend
When you're searching for the truth and it's right before your eyes
And somehow now you're able to see it but it's been there the entire time
When being disrespectful isn't cute and being cute isn't disrespectful
And after doing something wrong all of a sudden you're feeling regretful
When things you used to do you just don't want to do it anymore
Don't even start to panic you're just starting to mature
When your focus is off the streets and your focus is on a job
And you can walk down the street with worrying about a cop
When you decide yourself to those who dedicate themselves to you
And you stop harping on who's not around
And start embracing what's right in front of you
Everything is legit you have loyal friendships
And faithful and passionate loving relationships
Don't try to sabotage it, don't walk out the door
Don't even start to panic, you're just starting to mature

Conversations With LeAnn

Where have you been? Where are you now
Why didn't you come for me?
Why didn't you call me? Why didn't you at least
Write me some words that would comfort me?
Where have you been? Where are you now?
Why don't I hear from you?
It's been 6 years no contact at all!
No communication between us either
Where have you been? Where are you now?
I really have no clue
I've asked, I've wrote, I've called, I've hoped
And still no sign of you
Where have you been? Where are you now?
What do you plan to do?
What do you plan to do about the fact
That I'm still in love with you?
Where have you been? Where are you now?
Why can't I just let go?
You must not want me to know

Crazy I Admit

You ever had a bitch you couldn't depend on
Don't wanna fuck you on the regular but I'll expect you to come
home
Just feeling' like she entitled to some shit
Not understanding that you're very presence is a gift
Like bitch, I'm the prize
you lucky a nigga standing by your side
Compromising my pride and my stability
If a nigga went to jail or died
You probably wouldn't even remember me
On to the next on with their lives
Watch these bitches these hoes ain't right

Criminal

You hate me cause I fell in love
But for years I pretended
Speaking to your man, giving him hugs
Out of respect for you
I know he felt it
I know he seen how when you see me your eyes melted
Or how your smile grew
You loved me & everybody knew
But you were with him
Now was I mad at you
You say you love me but it be subliminal
Watching you give my love away
It's almost criminal

Dreaming

I dreamt of a woman who would love me forever
Who would never leave my side and cherish me as her treasure
My dream came true – but I'm dreaming again
Of a mother who is strong and determined to win
Will that dream ever come true
I most certainly don't have a clue
I'm dreaming again of freedom and a home
my freedom is coming my home I'll have to work for
but before I even finished that dream
I started dreaming for more
I'm dreaming of success, value and worth
I'm dreaming of belongings, and believing I'm not cursed
I'm dreaming of a life, one I never had
I'm dreaming of a man who I can call my dad
I'm dreaming of unity, strength and integrity
I'm dreaming of a future not letting the stress get the best of me
I'm dreaming of leadership and helping others like me
I'm dreaming of being someone I never thought I could be
I dream all day with my eyes wide open
I'm dreaming, I'm praying, I'm wishing, I'm hoping
I'm dreaming all night with my eyes shut tight
I'm dreaming of success throughout the rest of my life

Eazy

I guess I'll just let you go
Your mind is elsewhere
You're not the same as before

Facts

I try to be nice
Live life and do what's right
People make you want to fight
Sometimes kill
I'm often disliked because I keep it too real
Not accepting love that I only halfway feel
Friendships that constantly steal
Constantly take but never give
Friend that forget about all the things that you did
For them and their haters
Why is love and loyalty nowadays so rare
Family members treat you so unfair
Then make you feel obligated to be right there
Selfish people got my heart cold
My bright mind allows eyes to stare through your soul
Done being used I'd rather be alone
Fuck going out I'd rather stay at home
Then to be hanging around people who really want me gone
Acting like it's a right to do people so wrong
Division is best
My mind is my prize it's all I have left

Fallen Angels

I watched them carry out my sister in a body bag
They called me out to the hospital to go identify my dad
I saw my brother Guilian dead in the middle of Main Street
It sends chills down my spine every time I ride down 16th
Somewhere in my mind I thought Mrs. Hughley would always be
around
So when u heard she had died my whole mind spun around
Funeral after funeral my people are being buried
I know it killed Fat Fat when they killed his nigga Jerry
To see my sister lay in the bed
Holding my uncle Emory knowing he was dead
It really breaks my heart
Love is a bond you can't tear apart; some people can't be replaced
Some people just can't
Love it haunts you
It creates memories you can't erase

Goodbye

There will never be a goodbye maybe a see you later
We will always be united our love will only get greater
There will never be a goodbye, not a goodbye that I can see
I'll never leave you behind, it would be such a tragedy
They will never be a goodbye, not coming from these lips
I could never get you off my mind with your flawless legs and hips
There will never be a goodbye, you'll always hear from me
There will never be goodbye, not a goodbye that I can see

Heroin

She took the needle and hit herself
As she passed out I saw her
I thought she was about to die
She said "get off me baby you're ruining my high" Heroin

Hit Her Again

Her lip's were red, Her eyes were black
Her face was green and black,
Her finger's look as one as she took a drag or two off her cigarette
Her tears would fall.
I'd rub her back and listen to her sob
I'd say "I'm sorry this happened to you."
She just couldn't get him to stop
She'd say "He got mad and flipped out on me,
And beat me like I'm a man!"
He said "He'd changed, he loved me."
He promised he wouldn't hit me again
But he did it anyways
I swore I was done, I won't put up with this
She'd put him out without a problem
And just like that he was dismissed
As the hour's turned to day's and day's turned week's
She'd slowly start to miss him

He'd buy her gifts he'd called her
And come by and say things to make her want to kiss him
Within a few day's one's feeling kinda weak
She really needs her man
She'd let him back in
Swearing he'd changed and he'd never
Hit Her Again

Hopeless

Let's talk about what you did
How you crept in my soul and lived
How you made me feel like a god
To now when we lock eyes, not even a nod
Effortless sex
Wanting to connect
But no not for the nut
Just maybe she'll reach out and touch me today
Or maybe she'll look this way
Or smile at me and have something fulfilling to say
Hopeless romantic just wishing everyday

I

I'm really two people
I pretend I don't
But really I need you
Sick when I ain't see you
I wasn't able to keep you
Cause of her and what I allowed
So now onto you
Let's talk about what

Insanity

Is it weird that I feel at peace in here
Behind these walls in a cell
No answering calls or sellin' grams
Just for today I can relax
Nothings on my mind, I'm not watchin my back
But this is insane
I shouldn't feel like this
W.T.F. is wrong with my brain
I feel like prey out there
Everyday I'm a target
Racist ass yankees in a patrol car love to start shit
I got niggas that target cause I get to a check
But they really just hate me
Cause they know their bitch is next
I'm sittin' in this cell in Butler County Jail
With nothing on my brain
Not worried about a thang.

I Often Wonder

I often wonder what life would be like
For my mother
If she didn't take that pipe
And put that piece on that stem that one fatal night
That crack destroyed her life
Such a kind heart could have been anything in life
Shit wasn't right
Embarrassed by her failures one day she disappeared
She knew she had failed the one thing she had feared
But by this time she had kids
But the crack crept in her souls and that's where it lived
See try to understand
Cause I didn't but now I can
Understand how drugs make slaves out of men
And now that I'm no longer a child
I think to myself wow
I've watched the person I love the most
So easily put her life down
For the sake of others
Trying to gain acceptance from a society that hurt her
Instead of being a mother
But she was still somehow my best friend
Held me when I cried; cheered me on when I'd win
And for that Stephanie Lynn
I'll love you til the end

I Swear

I swear every time she wins
She comes through like the wind
Giving me love underneath my skin
Giving my face a grin
Making me feel
If I'm in pain it's her that heals
She like a pill
When I'm ill in the mind
When I'm weak shes my spine
Holding me up everytime
Then I wake up
And it's her I can't find
Her love was never mine
Maybe it was
Just on borrowed time
She's left me behind
Sweet memories of her divine
Love, comfort and time

I Take Pride in Mine

I take pride in mine, frontline for mine
What's beautiful is we all got a grind
I might be writing and Deshay might be modeling some of the time
Dontia in school and KeKe keep a job
So when they ask for anything it's never no prob
Or should I had said problem
If you talking G's, I got them
Think of my cousin EA
doing 20 years for slapping a bitch in the face
They say with a pistol
Them niggas was waiting on you to crash out G
They ain't really fuck with you
Since Tommy, Pooh, and Shadeed been gone
I can honestly say 16th doesn't feel like home
Just thinking about home

Justified Statistic 2

Am I the little girl lost, abandoned and neglected
Am I the drug dealer with diamonds in my necklace
Caster frames and Rolexes
Who am I
Am I a foreign car driver
Or am I a lonely soul with no one beside her
The provider, who'll never be provided for
Am I the one who wants a wife
Or want to run around and be a whore
Life is so obscure
Am I a poet destined for success
Or am I a poverty stricken mess
Trapped by a lifestyle
Glad I wasn't handed anything as a child
Cause they the type that's lazy
The beginning of the partnership was amazing
But we're not the same
See I'm a hustler, I don't think

He understand the game
Who am I
I guess you could say I'm a lost soul
Walking around on fire
But inside I'm so cold.

Justified Statistic 3

You couldn't stomach the things I've endured
In and out of detention walls and prison doors
Imagine watching someone physically lose their mind
Who was just fine but the time
The time was too harsh
Once where there was a ray of light
Its raw dark no hope
Imagine seeing your little brother gone off dope
My own niggas sellin it to him
I'm a gone head and put it out there
That was some shit I didn't feel
Carrying a concealed.

Untitled

I'm really two people
I pretend I don't
But really I need you
Sick when I can't see you
I wasn't able to keep you
Cause of her and what I allowed

I'm Somebody

I'm finally somebody, how excited am I
Somebody with a voice who does more than cry
Somebody with a goal, somebody with a plan
Somebody whose life will continue to expand
I'm finally somebody, how excited am I
Somebody with a dream far beyond the sky
I'm somebody who knows love no longer clutching pain
Somebody who has everything to lose and everything to gain
I'm finally someone who loves myself
Who nurtures and think and feels for herself
I'm finally somebody, how excited am I
Somebody with a voice who does more than cry

Intellectual Kisses

A life without pain is a life without purpose
What so we have to gain if we don't get below the surface
There's always room for growth but only if we choose
To open our eyes, listen to our hearts and examine what is true
Words can cut deep, but the pain will always pass
Only the strong will succeed and only the real will last
Success comes with a price, nothing good comes easy
You have to work to survive but the end result is pleasing
If you love it let it go, if it's real it'll come back
Be true to yourself and be careful who you attract
All money isn't good and some people may be toxic
If it's not something you understand, be careful not to knock it
I know you're tired of the storm
The clouds, they seem to fog your mind
But you'll come out it clear, refreshed and refined
Timing is always perfect
All that you dream will soon be reality
I know that it hurts
All that I've endured has taken a lot out of me
Life molds is and if we pay attention we come out of it strong
Be humble, walk proud and admit when you're wrong
Educate your mind, nurture your soul and listen to your spirit
I just thought I'd hand you a few of my intellectual kisses

Keeping Up Appearances

Screaming in my sleep at night, but no one seemed to hear
Bad nerves, cold sweats, nightmares and tears
Lost, confused, nowhere to go
With a lack of self- esteem
My helpless eyes, my lifeless smile, right there for them to see
Secrets keep you sick they say well just how I sick was I
40 years old men on top of me at the age of 5
Embarrassed, brainwashed, scared to tell, and scared to have no one
The same abuse repeating itself for years and years to come
Living in denial I would say nobody knew but me
But now I'm older hanging out with the man who molested me
Walking around smiling and joking like everything was fine
Haunting memories so vivid and real in the back of my mind
Am I sick?
I ask myself and wonder why I conceal it
Never telling anyone he took my spirit and killed it
Screaming through my eyes sometimes but no seemed to see
In disguise I walked around with the people who were hurting me

Laid Down

They laid me down
Danielle, hands up
They slammed me to the ground
I'm like what I do
They like We got a warrant out for you
We know what you do, we know what you sell
Highway patrol was like
Trumps in office so you know you goin' to jail
And for a very long time
Is this your 3rd strike yet
I'm like why you worried about my record
What I sell or what I do
If you was on the drug, I'd sell it to you too
But not because I want to, it's in demand
How dare you criticize us
When y'all putting it in our hands

Hearne House

Let's go deep
Let's talk about the fourteen-year-old who still had nightmares
Who was still pissing up her sheets cause in her mind
She's still scared
Although she knows he's not there
She knows he's not coming
But the thoughts in her mind make her sick to her stomach
Getting touched on and fucked on by her uncle as a youngin'
Nobody gonna believe her so she ain't saying nothing
Secrets keep you sick
I keep saying this
We gotta do better
She didn't have a chance cause no one let her

Lost Girls

You'll forever be a creep
A nigga might hit you up when everyone is asleep
I'm out here open the door type female
I gotta be somewhere early in the morning is the lie he tells
Man the shit you all believe
I mean the shit is wreck to me
With you he'll never be seen
Nothing more than a fuck
Might take you out to eat if he can spare a couple bucks
Won't speak to you in the club but might slide you a drink
Text you all night just to make sure shit sweet
Then down the line you wonder why you're alone
Creeping with niggas that had a girl at home
Fucking behind bitches that are supposed to be your friend
You will never have a real man
You will never have your own
Lost girls with no souls

Living Without you

It will only be a memory
Something we did
Something that was
Not something that is
Or will be
From the looks of things, you look happy to me
And me, CONSTANT GRIEF
Well not really
But I have these moments
When I wonder
If you think of me
Or what we could be
Or could've been
So close like kin
More years in but you moved on with him Damn... It hurts to think about it
Let me drink so I ain't got to think about it
It was a lot of nights I used to scream about it
Still trying to figure out how to live without it
Not it, I mean you
You. You. You.
Look at what you put me through
A nigga heart in two

Mary Louise Smith

I think about my Aunt Louise often
So when I do, I ride pass her old house on Crawford
Where rollup man and zooda queen used to live
I swear to God she used to torture us kids
With stories of Evil
She'd cuss you out good but I swear She was good people
and leave it up to Fat Fat to be her favorite.
I miss you, Louise Smith, I just had to come out and say it.

My dearest friend

Desperate, lonely, afraid I am
Of losing you
My friend, my confidant
Never judge me
Always for me, never against me
Even when I was against myself
I'm desperate to find you
Lonely cause you're gone
And afraid because
I'm desperate and alone

Bonnie

Overcome with guilt from my ignorance
Never taking out the time to apologize
Never willing to talk
Not wanting to forgive
Not caring enough to understand your reasons
I couldn't see things your way
I didn't want to
I wanted to stay upset
Stay hurt, be bitter
To me there was no good enough reason
No reason at all for why you cheated on me
For why I didn't get the chance I deserved
See then I didn't get it, but now I do
You made a choice to do nothing
To be nobody
To stay drunk and indulge in drugs
No food, no water sometimes
I barely had a place to live
You didn't care for me or yourself
Now I feel better because I know where you were
A place I'm not willing to go
A place I don't want to see
But now that you're gone
I wish I had a chance
Maybe to apologize
To try to understand
To not be overcome with guilt
From my ignorance

My Intention

My intention be to come home, kiss your lips and rub your thighs
Then lick the lips between and slide inside with this nine
But vibes
Them vibes be to the side
Throw my whole shit off
Now I'm laying here horny as I toss
Fuck turning
Wanna feel you cumming
Hear you yearning
But that attitude
Shit I shouldn't see out of you
You should be my biggest fan
My groupie
Supporting my dream
Not just giving me pussy

Neglect

For you to totally tell lies,
It gave me twisted thoughts.
I couldn't conceal my cries,
No matter what's the cost.
I walked around reckless,
Weeping from within.
From you're agonizing absence,
Time and time again.

People

People get up and carry on with their day

never considering the people that live to make their day carry on ......

#Be considerate of those you can call on it won't always be like that

12

*Police everywhere pulling us over giving out numbers calling us
names*
Then they put us in cuffs take us to court walk us in chains
Names like nuisance, menace, thug
All because you had no help and you had to sell some drugs
Not as a lifestyle but as a job
But they don't understand that on god
So they try to put us away
Mass incarceration is the new slavery anyway
Talking about drugs is in the way
But they putting in on the boat and delivering it right to your place
So what do you do when it's right there
And you don't have any shoes for school cause nobody cares
Open your eyes, stop being unaware
These people don't want us over here
But they keep us near
Uneducated slaves stuck in our ways
Just so they can sit back and wait to end our days

Poor Girl

In love with the idea of
who I thought your were
But now that I've grown
I see that you're not her.
Selfish, lonely, damaged and bitter
Now I see why no one stays with her
Babygirl you act like you're so much better
But you change niggas
More than the weather
And what is beauty without respect
You been wasted up baby
There's no more left

Mildred

I should've visited more
I should've sat and talked with you
Checked on you
Maybe sat back and watched a few black and white films
I could've picked up your groceries
Cleaned your house
I could've drove you around
Took you out to eat
I wished I had listened to you
Paid more attention
Stopped by more often
I wish I had created a stronger bond
I really should've swung on the porch with you
Combed your beautiful hair
Allowed you to reminisce
Listened to stories about your grandpa
I could've showed you I was present
That I was proud to be a part of you
I should've told you how thankful I was
I could've tried
But I didn't .... regret

RIP Mamas

When my grandma left there was nothing left
I mean no one
Go from feeling like you're everything everyday
Now to whom are you someone
To no one
Do you belong
No more protection from politics
Now i'm in children services and shit
With no one
Why did you leave
From a broken heart I truly believe
My angel my guide
It been one hell of a ride

Solo

You ever wanted to kill niggas
Cause you just don't feel niggas
Damn near no more real niggas
That's why I stay to myself
I ride and listen to music with no one else
With a 9 ruger or a 38 in my belt

She Worried

She worried about who you online talking to
Antennas don't work when it comes to the niggas that may be
plotting and stalking you
She'll sleep with your enemy
Take your money fuck your friend
And your dumb ass will still fuck with her
When you get out the pen
Guilt from the past
Creates a home with rare laughs
And much tension
You had two babies on her
Not to mention the two you had before
Now you call her a whore
Every time you look at the kid she had on you
When you had to go do your
Time in prison
Out here pretending
To keep up this image
Like y'all happy when y'all not
Just please y'all need to stop

Relationships Today

Sometimes it ain't nothing else to do but stop trying
Cause it's broke
And instead of standing there you gotta walk cause there's no hope
You fighting and trying
He cheating and lying
You on Facebook spying and for what
He knows you ain't gone leave so he really doesn't give a fuck
Yeah you'll be mad but you'll get over it quick
After a trip to the mall and a couple of outfits
Oh how quick we forget
How bad the heart is ripped when money is spent?
Then you wanna call a friend and vent
But she's tired of it so she doesn't wanna hear the shit
But she listens anyways
Even though her feeling about the situation are sideways
On love today
Shit just let us pray

Stay

Don't harm or hurt me
Heal me for the first time
Just feel me please
Let's live and love
I don't want you to leave

The Girl Inside of Me

Who cares for the little girl who was raped and molested
Who cares for the little girl who was abandoned and rejected
Who cares for the little girl who held resentment and anger
Who cares for the little girl who hitchhiked with strangers
Who cares for the little girl who constantly ran
Who cares for the little girl who was beat but still stands
Who cares for the little girl for her mom didn't even care
Who cares for the little girl whose dad was never there
Who cares for the little girl who got caught up in the system
Who cares for the little girl who started carrying pistols
Who cares for the little girl who made her own mistakes
Who cares for the little girl whose life was never safe
Who cares for the little girl who only wanted love
Who cares for the little girl who never held a grudge
Who cares for the little girl who didn't need an apology
Who cares for the little girl the girl who lives inside of me
Who cares for the little girl who always cared for everyone else
Who cares for the little girl who helped others and neglected herself
Who cares for the little girl who now sits in a prison cell
Who cares for the little girl who's destined by the system to fail
Who cares for the little girl who just wants her life to be okay
Who cares for the little girl who still struggles day to day
I care for the little girl, the girl that lives inside of me
I care for the little girl legend I am and will always be

The Reformatory

Brick walls, concrete floors, metal doors and steel bars
Gray shirts, black pants, cuffs and keys on prison guards
Count time, chow hall, commissary, and visitation
Get in a fight, conduct reports, hospital and segregation
Medium status, close status, max status, it's all the same
Drug infested men and women who play with recovery like it's all
a game
Homosexuals, lesbians, gays, whatever you want to call it
Little girls who look like boys are the specific target
Everybody looking for pity, looking for someone to love
Some trying to find a spot with the man from above
But it's all a con, it's all a game, it's all a big ass joke
Cause if heroin, meth or crack was around
They would all shoot and smoke
They build relationships with their kids
Only to leave and hurt them again
And wonder why the grow up mad
Not having a mother or a dad
It's a revolving door for some, many never seem to get right
This is just a brief description of everyday prison life

Hopefully

They call it a miserable existence
This life they live in
Those uncaged prisons
That hinder you in such a way
You can be living in poverty but still think it's okay
The mind of a slave
Slaves that don't know
Like her she's a hoe for dough
Legs stay open as long as the money flows
Slave
It's a frame of mind
But you'll get it in a matter of time
Hopefully

They Don't Know Me at All

They called me a liar and that not what I do
They called me a manipulator and that's not what I chose
They called me all types of shit that just isn't me
They called me a troublemaker because trouble made my rep
They said I played games and didn't have respect
They knocked me down constantly but in the end I stood tall
They smiled at my tears, gained strength when I was weak
20 haters against me, 20 haters I defeat
They played me to the left when I tried to treat them right
They broke my heart to pieces and played with my mind
They took away my freedom and robbed me of my time
They saw me as a nuisance who would do nothing but fall
It just goes to show that they don't know me at all
The drugs, the money, not even the girls define me
They judge from the outside never have they looked inside of me
I'm intelligent, giving, thoughtful, and charismatic
I love, I teach, I'm aggressive, and somewhat passive
I'm kind, I'm careful, I'm music and Im wind
I'm the feeling in your heart when you can't let go of him
So next time you see me take a good look at what you saw
Pay close attention and be sure because they don't know me at all

Beonca

This is a feeling I wish I could describe
I'd give you anything to look in your eyes, to hold your hand, to
hear your voice
Saying goodbye really wasn't my choice
And in my heart I know it wasn't your either
I knew when God said "come on"
You said "I don't want to leave her"
But I know you're not suffering anymore
So I guess I'll see you again when I walk through heaven's doors

To A Goddess

If I could picture heaven the gates would be your arms,
Welcoming me in safe and unalarmed.
Long road of gold leading me to your love,
I'd feel as I was floating on the cloud's from above.
If I could picture heaven it's your face that I would see,
With the eyes like diamonds shining down on me.
You're voice saying, "Come be with me forever."
Little do you know I'll follow you wherever.
You bring me to my knees as if I were to pray,
You're the reason why I breathe and wake up everyday.
So if were to picture heaven I would picture you,
With your everlasting love sitting on your pedestal.

Thoughts

What's on my mind
Never doing time
Having a family, I can call mine
Putting a smile on my mom's face one more time
Not to mention my book
Poetry got me hooked
Writing three at a time
Hoping maybe I won't have to sell dope somewhere down the line
I want my nephews lives to be better than mine
But how is that supposed to happen when they're constantly seeing crime
Kids out here fatherless
Just call them left behind
Makes me want to cry
But I smile
Nigga doesn't even understand it's an honor to have a child
Its hurtful when y'all not around
But fuck it

It is what it is

When I got out BG was so happy to see me
Took me shopping, put some shoes on my feet
Hold on don't let me sleep
How can I forget about them orgies on sixteenth
Some shit is bittersweet…
I was pressing up eight ounces on Kunz
Staring at dead bodies
Then I'd throw them in the truck and wait for everybody to call,
to come
So they could buy and I could sell
Chasing paper on the run
So I could pay a bill and they could get well
It's a fucked up cycle
When your own niggas don't like you
But they claim they love you
Just like the bitch did that fucked your brother
Sometimes I want to kill the niggas who sold dope to my mother
But what can I do
Sit in jail for life while she still does what she wants to do

Passionateless

Where's the passion
The passion is lacking
Why are you slacking
What the fuck happened
Shits coming unfastened
I'm steady trying to grab it
Make something happen
In the car crying to my nigga Magic
A lack of passion
Love and nurturing will have you real savage
Angry just out of habit
Cause the passion
Behind the words, the kiss
The hug, the pussy
Its everything I miss
I can't live passionate less

Wishful Thinking

I think of you often
I loved you from the start
I'll love you till the coffin
Our love was art
Man where do I start
Our memories kept me from falling apart
All that time we were apart
Love at first sight all over again
Even though I hadn't seen you in almost ten
Same smile so bright
With a swag to entice
Wish shit would have gone right
We talkin 2001
So 15 years as my wife
Wishful thinking; shit could've been so nice
But now,
I'm just dealing with life

Untitled #4

Should I care about jail
And who gone tell
Should time be a factor
When large amounts of money
is waiting for you after

20th Kid

Y'all niggas love RIP t-shirts
When if you would teach first
Maybe you wouldn't have to carry Little Larry in a hurst
And look at his mom, in so much pain that it hurts to look
I thought I recovered from being abandoned by you but it was
Something I never shook
Grew up without much so I learned how to cook crack
Me and Stevie was putting orajel on peanuts before that
Living in that little yellow house on 20th with the big tree in the
back
So many losses, I try not to think about that
I'm just a kid from The Sota I told you that
I told you what it was before all this happened man
Now you somewhere pissed cause your girl isn't your biggest fan
I told you
I took your girl and said let me mold you
And ain't shit about me local
Not from just around here, I'm also bicoastal
Have a nigga from another state come in and toast you

Cornball

You niggas really broke
Like damn pay people for that owed down dope
On Snapchat with Pelle coats
But your baby momma ain't got no soap
Guess that's your issue
But you'll buy the bar to impress
So niggas won't diss you
Shit don't make sense dude
Watered down and sweet like popsicles
Never overcoming any obstacle ass niggas
"I like to beat my bitch" fag ass niggas
Y'all some no class ass niggas
When I walk in the club and they don't know how to act
Don't know how to greet
Don't know whether to smile, stare or speak
Typical niggas
Hypocritical bitches
The niggas you grow up with end up snitching
Waking up every day wishing
Maybe praying
To the Gods
So many of them, my religion is at odds
So I keep my rod in my waist
And a little shank in a case to cut a nigga face
Dig a niggas grave
But AYE
Can you run that money this way

Act Of God

Your love is like the wind
Or the trees that kiss the sky
Your love is like the leaves in autumn before fall says goodbye
It's kind of like the sun that rises to warm the earth
Your love is like a wave in this ocean that I surf
Kind of like the calm right before the storm
Your love is all I need right here in my arms

Printed in the United States
By Bookmasters